# Learning
# Can Be Fun!

by Suzanne Briggs, MA

## Introductory Book

## Phonological Awareness

with Activities to Support

Structured Multisensory Language Programmes

P.22
Syll Snap.
P 25...
awareness of
Rime.
P.28

Egon Publishers Ltd

*Learning Can Be Fun!*
Introductory Book

Revised and enlarged edition 1999
Second Impression 2001
Second Edition 2010

Egon Publishers Ltd
618 Leeds Road, Outwood
Wakefield, West Yorkshire, WF1 2LT

Copyright (c) Suzanne Briggs

Illustrated by Rose using original ideas of
Nicky Robertson


ISBN 978 1 907656 002

# Contents

# Introduction

Research has proven that phonological awareness is a clear predictor of a child's ability to learn to read. Phonological awareness skills can be developed from Nursery age.

This book of structured phonological games and exercises has been devised to develop pupils' skills within an integrated programme, as an introduction to literacy at a pre-reading level. The games can be used in an enjoyable way as part of the daily language lessons.

Teachers and parents should use these games in the order that they are presented. The games follow a step by step training in phonological awareness using a multisensory approach. This encourages children to use all their sensory perceptual areas (visual, auditory, kinaesthetic – tactile) in an integrated way, which is essential for effective learning to take place.

The games provide reinforcement when learning and practice for all pupils, identifying those who have early difficulties in reading and spelling (e.g. those with Specific Learning Difficulties, i.e. Dyslexia). The games in 'Alphabet Sequencing' and 'Word Attack Skills' ('Learning Can Be Fun!' Books 1 & 2) should be introduced at the same time.

The author has worked for over 30 years with pupils with Specific Learning Difficulties and was co-editor of 'The Hickey Multisensory Language Course' – 2nd Edition, 1992. Her research (Briggs, 1997) was based on the 'Management and Transfer of Structured Language Teaching to the Classroom' and has successfully benefited all children in the classroom. As a tutor and trainer of teachers, she has shown how the classroom teacher can identify and help children with learning difficulties, including those who are bilingual, by using these games. The exercises and games in this series of books have been collected over a number of years from teachers following specialist courses and several were included in the second edition of the Hickey Course.

# Phonological Awareness

**Research** carried out in the UK, USA and Scandinavia in the last thirty years, has shown that phonological awareness is a clear predictor of a pupil's ability to cope with the early stages of learning to read (Vellutino, 1987, 1996). Phonological awareness is a linguistic ability to segment words into their constituent units of sound (e.g. phonemes). The first stages in literacy teaching in this book are introduced with the use of objects and pictures, providing interest with vital language and listening training at the pre-reading level. When these skills are more developed, then the use of alphabetic symbols is introduced.

## Deficits in basic reading skills

There is a wealth of evidence to show that deficits in phonological processing not only occur together with deficits in basic reading skills but are causal in preventing the acquisition of these skills (Lundberg et al, 1988; Torgesen, 2000). Analysis of phonemes is more predictive of a skill in reading (Blachman, 1988; Goswami, 1996; Shaywitz, 2003) and develops at a later stage.

## Phonological processing

The research defines the close association of the development of speech, language and phonological processing, and the influence that this has on a child's ability to learn to read and spell. It has been described as encompassing several skills at each developmental stage, beginning with phonological awareness in rhyme and is closely related to spoken language in the early stages of development. Liberman (1978; Foy & Mann, 2001) suggested that phonemic awareness develops between the ages of 5-6 years. She said that it was exceptional for a child to succeed in counting phonemes, in a phoneme counting task, before this age, however, 70% of 6-7 year olds showed no difficulty with either task.

## 'Orthography' is a study of spelling

Children who are not consciously aware of the segments of phonemes in speech, may not be able to hear rhyme and are unable to hold the segments in their memory to be compared, analysed or ordered (Lindamood et al, 1997). English orthography is based on an alphabetic code and relies on phonological awareness.

## Problems in processing the speech sounds

Problems in processing the speech sounds occur when children have not developed a phonological awareness of speech sounds. Although this is frequently evident in children who have had delayed speech in the early years, it can also occur in children who appear to have had no difficulties and have spoken quite clearly from an early age. A child needs a good command of a spoken first language before starting school. When learning to read, the processing of spoken language needs to be integrated with a system for processing written language (Goswami & Bryant, 1990; Snowling et al, 1994). Children who speak more than one language in their early years may not be so proficient in their first language.

## Short-term memory deficit

Problems with phoneme segmentation and synthesis (i.e. combining parts of a word into a complete whole) also result in difficulties in accessing and activating phonological memory codes. Evidence of phonological short-term memory can be seen in the results of the Digit Span Test (WISC/Aston Index). It affects the ability to concentrate and retain information in the auditory short-term memory, in order to process it effectively.

## Stages of literacy development

In a model of literacy development Frith (1985) explained that children move through three phases of development:

i) **The logographic stage** (initial whole word recognition – spoken words leading to written letters in whole words).

ii) **The alphabetic stage** (letter-sound correspondences). The key stage, according to Frith (1985), is the 'alphabetic stage' which relies on phonological processing in speech and language. There are two levels at this stage, initial and advanced.

iii) **The orthographic stage.** Larger units can be segmented, leading to automaticity in reading and spelling words with long vowel sounds and the study and use of morphemes. Morphemes deal with the origins and meaning of words by studying the roots, prefixes and suffixes.

**The games and exercises in this book follow the Frith model.**

## Children with literacy difficulties (dyslexia)

The failure to progress through the stages is characteristic of children with literacy difficulties, such as 'dyslexia', who may compensate by using any stage, at any time, but none very efficiently. Children who have difficulty with written language skills, have difficulty in progressing though the 'alphabetic stage' when learning to read. This is caused by their difficulties with sound/symbol association due to poor phonological awareness. They have an inability to use alphabetic coding skills correctly (Snowling & Hayiou-Thomas, 2006). Although many children overcome their early difficulties with reading, they will always have difficulties with spelling and transferring their ideas to paper when writing. The rate at which they process information and their ability to cope under the pressure of examinations is also affected. These children need structured language teaching to learn to read and spell. A structured multisensory approach through writing is essential for dyslexic children and those with literacy difficulties.

# Stages of literacy development

## 2-3 years – Rhyming

Awareness of rhyme is the stage before developing phonemic awareness (Bryant et al, 1990). The scores that were obtained from rhyme detection tests indicated that children's sensitivity to rhyme reflects on their ability to make analogies (Goswami, 1996) and also their learning of spelling patterns. There is evidence that sensitivity to nursery rhyme in pre-reading children of 3 years can be stimulated by a rich linguistic environment. This improves the rate of learning by increasing the use of the strategy for spelling by analogy. 'Rhyme' refers to words that have similar sounds but may have different spellings, e.g. 'bear', 'there', 'hair', 'care'.

## 3-4 years – Syllable segmentation

The next stage demonstrated by the research of Liberman et al (1974), was with children at the pre-reading stage. A syllable task showed that 3-4 year olds can divide a stream of speech sounds into syllables, e.g. 'buttercup' - 'but' / 'ter' / 'cup', showing their awareness of syllables and the constituent parts of words.

## 4-5 years – Onset and rime

There are around 800 families of rhyming words in English, and most of them have consistent 'rime' spelling patterns. Bradley & Bryant (1978) realised that the ability to segment syllables into onset and rime, and then link phonemes to blend letters in words, demonstrated a step by step procedure in the development of reading and spelling. 'Onset' refers to the first consonants and 'rime' refers to the following vowel and consonants, e.g. in the word 'spin', 'sp-' is the onset and '-in' is the rime. Examples of other words in this rime group are 'pin', 'din', 'tin'. There are 884 words that share a rime with 'in'. Children who cannot read whole words effortlessly, cannot use analogy to compare words of similar spelling patterns as in 'oat', 'boat', 'coat', 'goat' (Vellutino, 1979; Goswami, 1996; Stackhouse & Wells, 1997). Children need to be given a strategy based on onset and rime to attack new words, before they are expected to segment phonemes.

## 5-6 years – Phoneme segmentation

Children who automatically see letters and recognise the sounds as wholes are able to see words as patterns of letters. They learn to read with little difficulty. Children who do not have this ability need to follow a structured multisensory language course, with clue pictures to learn to visualize and link individual letters and their shapes to sounds (Treiman et al., 1997, 2002). For these children (i.e. dyslexics) learning to read and spell will not be an automatic process. More severe difficulties are evident when encoding sounds for spelling, as this is more complicated and requires efficient linguistic use of phonological processing skills (Frith, 1985; Snowling, 1987, 1995).

## Use of analogy (e.g. making comparisons)

Children's reading and spelling skills progress more quickly when they are able to form analogies between familiar words and non-words (Goswami, 1996). They appear to learn more effectively when onset and rime is taught alongside syllable segmentation (Snowling et al, 1994; Adams, 1990). When taught the spelling pattern of one word children need the ability to transfer this spelling information about the rime to another word. Dyslexics have particular difficulty decoding non-words. Snowling (1995) devised a non-word test as a part of her research and this test may be used to identify a specific learning difficulty.

## Stages in developing phonological awareness

There are a number of stages that the teacher can check and develop in school before beginning formal teaching of reading (Gillon, 2004). The stages in phonological awareness training are:

1. Ability to listen
2. Awareness of rhyme
3. Syllable segmentation
4. Use of 'rime' in words
5. Alliteration and identification of 'onset' sounds in words
6. Awareness of the position of the vowel sounds
7. Phoneme segmentation and deletion

## Screening and assessment procedures

In the UK, a Baseline Screening Assessment is used with all children on entry to Reception Year classes (rising 5 years).

(See Resources, p.57 for references to testing materials for phonological awareness.)

# The Logographic Stage

## 1. LEARNING TO LISTEN

Many children go to playgroups and nursery groups before they start school. Some do neither but start school at Reception age (in the UK 4+ years). They will all come to school from very varied backgrounds and at different stages of development. Some have had more parental attention than others with spoken language, rhymes and songs. Shared enjoyment in books may have been introduced from four months of age and they may have started to learn to concentrate and attend to sounds in language and words. Others may not have had the opportunity to develop these listening skills.

### Listening is an active skill

Frost (1998) said that the aim is to work with the children's control of their own attention. He explained that language awareness is built on the ability to focus attention towards something which the child has chosen as a target for that attention. Before children are ready to be introduced to symbols for reading and spelling, there may be much work to be done to develop listening skills and awareness of sounds. Structured games should be played to check and train children's ability to listen to the sounds around them, before any formal reading is introduced. Too many teachers expect children to understand the meaning of a 'sound' when introducing a symbol (e.g. a letter of the alphabet).

### The six developmental stages of attention

As listening requires attention, teachers and parents need to be aware of the six developmental stages of attention control, observed by Reynell (1977, 1978) and referred to by speech therapists. It is important to recognise children's attention difficulties early. Children's attention levels can be recognised in the first term of school. Many can soon overcome their difficulties by following a quiet five minute attention programme each day, which is obtained from a speech therapist. Parents can follow this up at home.

| | | |
|---|---|---|
| Level 1 | Extreme distractibility and fleeting attention | (up to 1yr) |
| Level 2 | Rigid attention to own choice of activity | (1-2 yrs) |
| Level 3 | Single channelled internal attention, i.e. will attend to adult's choice of activity only under adult's control | (2-3 yrs) |
| Level 4 | Single channelled attention under child's control means the child will continue an activity introduced by an adult but is still easily distracted | (3-4 yrs) |
| Level 5 | Integrated attention for short spells. Child is able to concentrate on adult, while playing with another toy | (4-5 yrs) |
| Level 6 | Integrated attention – well controlled and sustained | (5-6 yrs) |

# 2. GAMES TO DEVELOP LISTENING SKILLS

Listening requires the use of language to describe sounds that can be heard.
The skills required in order to learn to listen, are the ability to:

    i.    select and focus attention
    ii.   concentrate attention
    iii.  discriminate
    iv.  sequence and retain auditory information
    v.   use auditory and visual information together
    vi.  use language and describe what is heard

## i. Ability to select and focus attention

– Talk about sounds that can be heard in the room.
– Do this with eyes open and then eyes closed and discuss which is the easier way to listen.
– Talk about sounds heard outside the room.
– Listen and talk about body sounds heard internally.
– Talk about why we have sounds; do we need them?
  Which sounds can be comforting or worrying?

## ii. Concentrate attention

– Listen to loud or quiet sounds and use language to describe them.
– Listen to sounds with high or low notes and different tones, harsh, soft or smooth, etc.
– Identify sounds on a tape recording (e.g. animals, bird song, kitchen noises).
– Use musical instruments. The teacher (or children) plays an instrument(s) in different parts of the room, while others say where they can hear the sounds.
– Listen to an individual instrument, then listen to music and identify when the instrument is played (e.g. 'Peter and the Wolf').
– Play guessing games with eyes open and then closed. A child standing behind a curtain or sheet picks up an object for the other children to guess and name (e.g. bell, buzzer, chime bars, rattle).
– Guess a sound made with eyes closed (e.g. a door closing, footsteps, sipping from a cup, cutting with scissors, sharpening a pencil, dropping something, turning a page, water dripping).
– Guess an action (e.g. a sniff, cough or sneeze, puffing or panting, scratching).

## iii. Ability to discriminate

– Some children find it very difficult to direct their attention towards speech and articulation at the same time as hearing and seeing.
– Use pictures and words with similar initial sounds (bin, pin) and the child says 'same' or 'different'. Also do the same with final sounds.
– Use tests for auditory discrimination (e.g. 'Aston Index' or 'Hornsby').
– Play 'Chinese Whispers'. First player whispers a message (e.g. "In the deepest of bogs you will frighten frogs") to next player and this is repeated around the circle. Final player says the message s/he received to all.

## iv. Ability to sequence and retain auditory information

- Make two sounds and ask the children to tell you what they are. One child can repeat them (e.g. clap hands, stamp on floor).
- When confident move onto three sounds (e.g. rub hands, sniff, cough).
- Make three sounds, give an instruction (e.g. close the door or draw a cat) and then ask the children to identify the sequence of sounds.
- Move onto four sounds. Name sounds in order. Repeat but leave one sound out (e.g. tear paper, close a book, drop something, cough). Alternatively try adding sounds to the list.
- Play *'The Head Teacher's Cat'*. Describe the cat, first player choosing a word stating with letter 'a', second player with 'b' etc. right up to 'z'. Each player must repeat the words in order from the previous players before adding a new word beginning with the next letter of the alphabet.

## v. Using auditory and visual information together

- Give a sequence of action tasks (e.g. put the pencils on the chair, those books on the floor and then close the door).
- Make tape recordings of three to four sounds. Give the children a set of cards with sound matching pictures. Ask them to order the pictures from the sounds heard.
- Give three to five pictures for a story. Ask the children to listen to the sounds on the tape and put the pictures in order.

## vi. Ability to use language and describe what is heard

This involves the use of visual and auditory memory.

- Children move when they hear the name of their character read out in a story.
- A story is told by the teacher and retold by the children in turn.
- Mirror pictures. First child has paper and coloured pencils. Second child has a picture to describe. Second child explains the picture to first child who draws the picture.
- Use a 'secret bag' to feel and name an object. Can they describe it to the others without naming it first?
- Take the 'secret bag' home and find a sound to bring to school (this will involve the family). Keep it a secret? Children try to guess it before the sound is made. Is it a high / low or loud / quiet (etc.) sound? Can it make other sounds? Why does it make this sound?

# 3. LISTENING TO RHYME

Children begin to learn about the phonological structure of language (Bryant & Goswami, 1990; Muter et al., 1997) by playing with rhyme. Rhyme is a vital early stage of linguistic development in spoken language from two years. Bryant & Bradley (1987) showed that children from two years can judge that two words rhyme. Beginner readers need to be phonologically aware of rhyme before they can segment speech sounds in words. The use of rhyme shows that phonological awareness is evident in some pre-readers (Fox & Routh, 1976; Goswami, 1995). Lundberg, Frost & Petersen (1988) have shown that phonological awareness can be trained before any formal instruction in reading is given, in their research in Scandinavia with six year old children. Blachman (1991) said that this training should be included in all pre-school curriculum programmes, especially for children who have consistently poor rhyming skills in the pre-school years.

## Sequences of development:

i.   Only use objects and pictures in the initial stages to develop an awareness of sounds with rhyme.

ii.  The use of rhyme should be introduced using action, music and rhythm.

iii. The sequence of development from the use of objects and pictures (visual/kinaesthetic) follows to singing and listening to rhymes (auditory) and rhythm (mentioned on previous pages).

## Suggestions for rhyming activities

### Game 1: Missing nursery rhymes

**To play:** These can be sung and acted out in class and in music lessons. The teacher starts a nursery rhyme but leaves out the rhyming word for the children to complete, e.g.

'Jack and Jill

Went up the ....

14

## Game 2:  Number rhyming games

**To play**:  These can also be used in the same way with matching picture cards for the rhyming word, e.g.

| | |
|---|---|
| One, two, buckle my .... | (shoe) |
| Three, four, knock at the ..... | (door) |
| Five, six, pick up .... | (sticks) |
| Seven, eight, lay them .... | (straight) |
| Nine, ten, a big fat .... | (hen) |

## Game 3:  Rhyming name pairs

**To play**:  Make up rhyming pairs using children's names, e.g.

| | |
|---|---|
| 'Her name's Sally, she lives in the .... | (valley) |
| 'His name's Hugh, he hates .... | (stew) |
| 'Little Mike, rode his big .... | (bike) |

## Game 4:  Playground rhythm and rhymes

**To play**:  Bring back and make up playground rhythm games.  The children clap, skip, and hop to the rhythm of the rhyme, e.g.

'Dan, Dan was a silly old man,
He washed his face in a frying pan,
He brushed his hair with a fox's tail,
And scratched his tummy with a big toe nail'

(See *'The Lore and Language of Schoolchildren'* by Iona & Peter Opie)

'Mary had jam, Mary had jelly,
Mary went home with a pain in her .....(?)
Now don't be mistaken, don't be misled
Mary went home with a pain in the .....(?)

## Game 5:  Counting out rhymes

'Eeny Meeny Miney Mo,
Catch a tiger by his toe,
If he squeals let him go,
Eeny Meeny Miney Mo,
O – u – t spells out,
So out you must go.'

## Game 6: 'A Hunting We Will Go' (Song)

**To play:** Enlarge and photocopy the pictures on the next page onto card (and colour).

- The children sit in a circle or group.

- They are each given a picture card with the rhyming word for the song, e.g.

  'A hunting we will go
  A hunting we will go
  To catch a fox
  And put it in the ....'        (box)

- The children can collect more rhyming words for this song and pictures are then drawn, e.g.

| 'To catch a dog | - | standing on a log' |
|---|---|---|
| '....    cat | - | sitting on a mat' |
| '....    pig | - | wearing a wig' |
| '....    mouse | - | running in the house' |
| '....    rat | - | eating a hat' |
| '....    fish | - | put it on a dish' |
| '....    shark | - | hiding in the dark' |
| '....    gnu | - | sitting on the loo' |
| '....    flea | - | chasing a bee' |

# Pictures for song 'A Hunting We Will Go'
(Enlarge and photocopy for group or class use)

## Game 7: The 'Basket games'

**Prepare:** Collect a number of objects to put into a small basket.

- Suggested objects to collect for the rhyming basket – car, boat, ball, spoon, pen, stick, peg, pin, clip, pad, cat, brush, sheep, book, sock.

**To play:** 'Rhyming Game'

- The children select an object from the basket. They name it and give a rhyming word.
- Counters can be used to score points.
- Extra points can be scored if other matching, rhyming words can be given.
- Objects can also be put into a 'Feely Bag' and a child gives a rhyme for the other children to guess the name of the object.

## Game 8:  Toss the ball

**Prepare:**  Soft ball or bean bag.  List of words to use for the game

**To play:**  The children stand in a circle with the teacher, who gives a word
e.g. 'goat'.

- The soft ball (or bean bag) is tossed to someone in the circle who gives a
  rhyming word, e.g. 'float', and then tossed quickly to someone else as the game
  continues.

- Five rhyming words can be given before moving on to the next sound.

- Alternatively a scorer can count to see how many rhyming words are given for
  each sound.

| goat | meet | gate | slime |
| boat | street | mate | mime |
| stoat | fleet | rate | rime |
| float | sleet | slate | time |
| moat | sweet | Kate | lime |

| spoon | tall | eel | Pope |
| soon | small | feel | rope |
| baboon | hall | wheel | hope |
| cocoon | wall | heel | slope |
| goon | call | kneel | cope |

## Game 9:  Silly rhyming sentences

**To play:**  These can be given as a listening game for the children to complete,
Examples:

| | |
|---|---|
| 'The man in jail got some .... | (mail) |
| 'The funny seal ate his ... | (meal) |
| 'The bad dream made him | (scream) |
| 'I fell out of bed and hurt my ... | (head) |
| 'Take a look at my new ... | (book) |
| 'Look at Fred, he is still in ... | (bed) |
| 'That greedy goat is eating my ... | (coat) |
| 'The big brown bear sat in my ... | (chair) |
| 'I saw a pig eating a ... | (fig) |
| 'The amazing shark is trying to ... | (bark) |
| 'My mum bakes lovely chocolate ... | (cakes) |
| 'Who put that rock into my ... | (sock) |

## Game 10: Missing rhyme hunt

**To play:**  The teacher gives a sentence with a non-rhyming word and the children change it.

Examples:

| | |
|---|---|
| 'I am a mole and I live in a <u>house</u>.' | (hole) |
| 'I have a car but it won't drive <u>a long way</u>.' | (far) |
| 'I have a cat that sits on the <u>rug</u>.' | (mat) |
| 'Sam gets a shiver when he swims in the <u>stream</u>.' | (river) |
| 'The little chick sat on a <u>twig</u>.' | (stick) |
| 'The soup was so thick it made me <u>ill</u>.' | (sick) |
| 'Ben found a snake in the big <u>pond</u>.' | (lake) |

- Encourage the children to make up their own missing rhymes.

(See Resources List, p.57 for further ideas)

## 4. SYLLABLE SEGMENTATION

Phonological awareness for syllables and syllable 'tapping', precedes that for phonemes (Wagner & Torgesen, 1987; Wolf et al., 2000). It develops between 3 and 5 years before the stage when children are taught to read. Children can segment syllables in words before they can segment phonemes. The segmentation of syllables in words may be followed by at least one stage before segmenting phonemes, which young children find difficult before 5-6 years (Treiman, 1985, 1992; Bourassa & Treiman, 2003). Games need to be played to give practice and experience in segmenting syllables in words. All these games use a multisensory approach to learning. They also help to develop pupils' expressive language, visual and auditory short-term and observational skills.

### 'Basket Games'

**Prepare:** Collect a number of objects to put into a small basket with 1, 2, 3, 4 or more syllables in their names, e.g. yo-yo, handkerchief, rhinoceros.

- Make a set of cards numbered 1 to 5.

- Find a games board, cloth bag and a small tray.

### Game 1: 'Name game'

**To play:** This is an excellent game for use of language. Discuss the names of the objects in the basket and then beat out the syllables in each word.

- Children select an object and give the name. They clap their hands for each syllable in the word. Can another word be given for the object?

- Use children's names or names of animals, fruit and vegetables etc. to tap out the syllables. Children who find the tapping task difficult can use a set of blocks when counting.

21

*called basket of toys*

## Game 2: 'Syllable snap'

**To play:** The caller has a set of 5 cards numbered from 1 to 5. *or dice*

*good*
- The pupils are given five toys each from the basket.
- The caller holds up a number card.
- The pupils win a point if they show their toy with the same number of syllables and say 'SNAP'.

*caterpillar*
*butterfly* *ball* *both* *robot,* *ruler*
*car* *dice* *cow,* *paint brush*
*dinosaur* *car* *pig* *teddy bear*
*notepad* *spoon*

## Game 3: 'Feely bag'

**To play:** Put 5 - 10 objects into a bag.
- First player feels for an object and gives the number of syllables in the name.
- The other children guess what it is and give the name.

## Game 4: 'I-Spy'

**To play:** Put 10 objects, each with 2 - 4 syllables in its name, onto a tray.
- First player looks at the objects and says, "I-spy something with 2 syllables", etc.

## Game 5: 'Kim's game'

**Prepare:** Put 5 -10 objects on a tray. The pupils study the objects and the tray is covered. The game can be played in a number of ways:

**To play:** a) Ask the pupils to memorise all the objects with one syllable (or more) <u>or</u>
b) Remove one object. The pupils identify the missing object.

## Game 6: 'Three in a line' *Make*

**Prepare:** Make a large 'Noughts and Crosses' board. You will need a basket of objects with 2 and 3 syllable words.

*ok*
*good*
**To play:** A game for two players or two teams.
- Objects are used from the basket with 2 or 3 syllables.
- Each player decides which to have. First player takes an object from the basket and counts the syllables. Next player follows.
- The first player with 2 or 3 syllables in a line wins.

## Game 7: 'Double your number'

**Prepare:** A games board (see next page). This may be coloured in by the pupils, or they may draw their own board. A basket of objects with multi-syllable names.

**To play:** The pupils play in turn.
- Points are scored for the syllables counted in the name of the object, taken from the basket.
- Extra points may be scored if the pupil can extend the description and total the number of syllables used, e.g. 'yellow yo-yo' (4 syllables).
- The pupils can 'double their number' if correct.

# 5. VISUAL SHORT-TERM MEMORY

## Game: 'Pairs' or 'Memory'

This game can be adapted to play many word games. It can also be played for syllable segmentation games using syllable picture cards. (Pictures can be taken from 'Learning Can Be Fun' – Book 2.)

**Prepare:**

- Make 10 pairs of cards with '1' on the reverse of the first card and '2' on the second.
- Put a different picture with the same number of syllables on the face of each pair. or as below, the matching initial letter is printed on card 2.

Use picture pairs with 1 to 5 syllable words.

**To play:** Put all cards face down on the table.

- First player turns over a '1' and a '2' card in its place on the table.
- If each card has a picture that matches the number of syllables on the other card, or the matching initial letter, the player wins the pair.
- Play continues until all cards have been taken. The game may finish after a player has won three sets.

The rules for the game can be adapted to the time allowed.

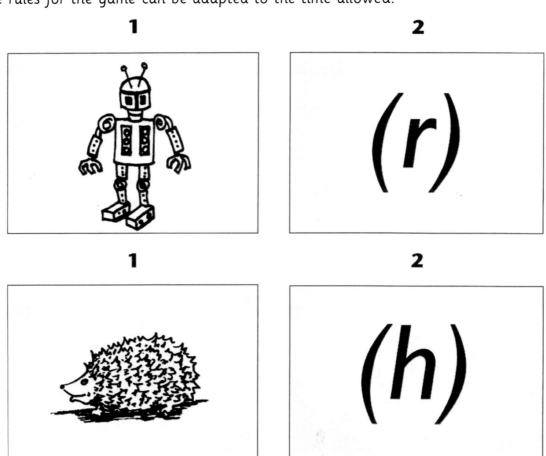

# Initial Alphabetic Stage

## 1. ONSET AND RIME

Treiman's (1985, 2002) suggestion that young children's phonemic awareness at this stage should be described in terms of 'onset and rime' is supported by the fact that pre-readers do have remarkable early rhyming skills. The 'onset' in a word is an initial consonant or consonant cluster and a 'rime' is the vowel and any following consonants, e.g. the onset in 'strand' is 'str', the rime is 'and'. Treiman's research drew attention to children who, at the age of five years, could segment words more easily into 'onset' and 'rime' before they could segment words into single phonemes. In running speech, letters in a syllable overlap are on top of each other, making it difficult for the ear to separate them (Liberman et al, 1989). Goswami (1996) agreed with Treiman (1985) that the onset and rime stage of analysis in young children precedes the phoneme segmentation stage.

## 2. AWARENESS OF RIME

### Game 1: 'Picture sort'

**Prepare:** Photocopy each picture on the following pages onto card. Enlarge pictures if working with younger children or a larger group.

**To play:** Discuss and establish with the children, the name to be given to each picture for the sets of words with a similar rime (e.g. sip, hip, snip, tip). Do not give them any information or reason.

Establish the names of the pictures as follows:

| tip | sip | hip | snip | nit | pit | hit | sit |
|-----|-----|-----|------|-----|-----|-----|-----|
| tin | pin | spin | din | tap | map | lap | nap |
| man | pan | tan | Dan | Dad | sad | mad | pad |

**First stage:** Give each group of pupils a set of words (4 with the same rime).

• They sort their pictures into sets.
• Ask them to explain how they have sorted their cards.
The aim is to see if they can identify the 'rime' in the picture words.

**Second stage:** Give out cards with similar rimes but with one card that does not match.

• Ask the pupils to talk in their groups about their pictures, to discover how to sort them.
• Why does one card not match or belong to their set?

# Onset and rime pictures

# Onset and rime pictures

## Game 2:  'Win a picture set' – 'twos' or 'fours'

**Prepare:**  One pack of picture cards prepared as for previous game.  One set of rime cards to match the picture cards, e.g. '- it', '- ip'. '-an', '-at', '-ap'.  Picture cards are matched to the cards with the letters for the rimes.

**To play:**  Place the rime cards on the table, face up.

- Place the picture cards in the pool, face down.
- First player takes a picture card, gives the name of the picture and the rime, e.g. 'sit, -it'.
- The picture is placed in the column under the '-it' card.
- The player who puts down the 2nd or 4th card wins those cards in the rime set and play continues.

## Game 3:  'Odds and evens'

**Prepare:**  One pack of rime picture cards as prepared for previous game.  One dice.

- Make dice cards with the rimes of the words that are in the picture pack and put two rimes onto a dice card.  *(See below).

**To play:**  Throw the dice.  A player finds a picture card to match the rimes on their dice card.

- The first to collect three pictures of a kind wins the game.

+ dice

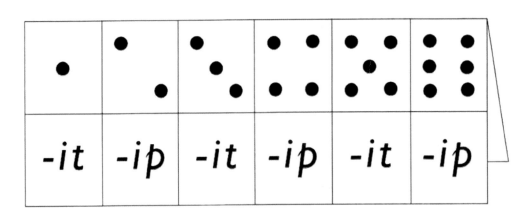

* '-it' is used for odd numbers and '-ip' for even numbers.

# 3. AWARENESS OF ONSET

## Game 4: 'Eureka'

**Prepare**: A game using alliteration to identify, isolate and match the onset, (i.e. initial) sounds of words. (See pictures on the next page.)

Sets of 4 picture cards with similar initial sounds, plus one card that is different. Examples:

| | | | | |
|---|---|---|---|---|
| sea | sun | sand | sail | (boot) |
| tin | top | tan | tap | (dog) |
| pin | pot | pig | pop | (cat) |
| nip | nut | nail | nest | (bird) |
| dog | dot | door | dart | (mat) |

**To play:**

**First stage**: Give each group of pupils a set of words. The pupils are encouraged to discover how their pictures can be sorted into their similar sets. The aim is to see if they can identify the 'onset' in the picture words.

**Second stage**: Give cards to each group with similar 'onsets' but with one card that does not match. Ask the pupils to talk about their pictures and discover which card is the odd one out.

**Third stage**: Give each group one picture. They are asked to give 4 words with a matching 'onset' and all call out 'Eureka' when they have done it. If the 'onset' is a single letter, e.g. 's' then all words must begin with 's', not an initial blend (e.g. 'st', 'sl', 'sn', etc.).

**Fourth stage**: Give each child a picture. Show the children an 'onset' letter and they hold up their picture cards that match the 'onset' letter.

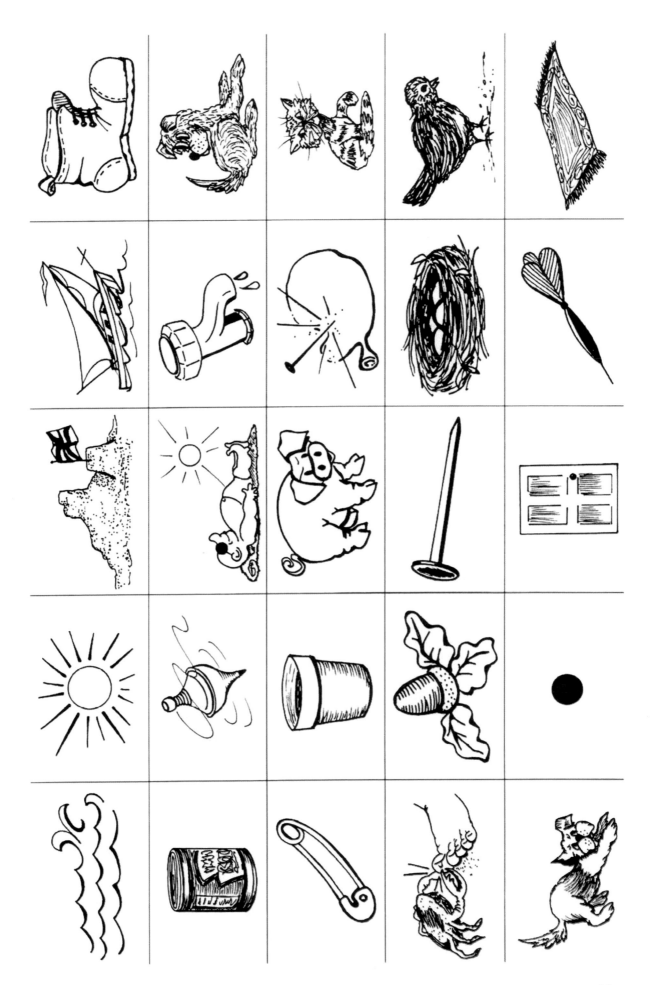

30

## Game 5: 'Crack the code'

**Prepare:** A set of individual pictures with each card representing an initial, medial or final sound in the alphabet, e.g. 'sun (s)', 'apple (a)', 'nut (n)', 'dog (d)', 'pig (p)', 'igloo (i)', 'tent (t)', 'hat (h)'. The letter(s) for each picture is/are printed on the reverse of the card.

- Put the printed letter on the face of the card. These can be used as cue cards for group or individual memory training of the sounds of the phonemes. The cards can be enlarged and photocopied.

- The aim is for the children to give a quick response when they see the letter on the face of the card, by responding with the cue picture and sound it identifies, e.g. sun (s).

**To play:** When the children are aware of onset sounds in words. They can work in groups with sets of these cards.

- They make up their own picture words by saying a word, e.g. 'sip' and taking a picture for each sound they hear in the word.
  (See below)

*photoc*

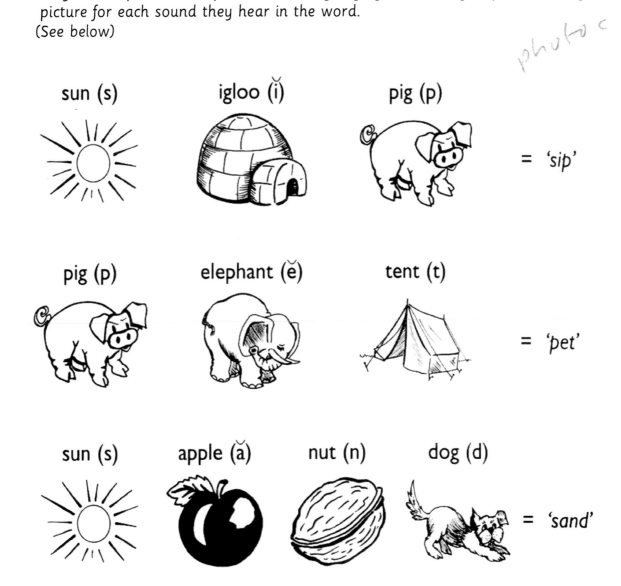

sun (s)   igloo (ĭ)   pig (p)   = 'sip'

pig (p)   elephant (ĕ)   tent (t)   = 'pet'

sun (s)   apple (ă)   nut (n)   dog (d)   = 'sand'

# Memory cards for phoneme practice and 'crack the code' games
## Put printed letters for clue words on reverse side of each card

sun (s)

apple (ă)

nut (n)

dog (d)

pig (p)

hat (h)

elephant (ĕ)

cat (k)

leg (l)

boy (b)

monster (m)

umbrella (ŭ)

jug (j)

girl (g)

fish (f)

yoyo (y)

king (k)

duck (k)

orange (ŏ)

rug (r)

van (v)

watch (w)

zebra (z)

queen (kw)

box (ks)

thumb (th)

shop (sh)

chat (ch)

book (o͝o)

moon (o͞o)

sweet (ē)

ball (l)

## 4. BLENDING SOUNDS

### Game 6: 'The train games'

The challenge of playing a game can make the difficult task of learning to blend sounds together to read words more enjoyable. This game is used to give pupils practice in blending sounds and also helps to develop their skill in using words with onset and rime. The 'train game' can be adapted for all levels of sounds in words, to encourage word-building and for reading practice, e.g.

i) short vowel sounds

ii) initial and final blends, e.g. ball, hall, call, fall, etc.

iii) vowel-consonant-e words, e.g. cake, rake, bake, make, etc.

iv) vowel digraphs, e.g. rain, pain, main, train, etc.

v) multi syllable words

The trains can be extended to have as many carriages as necessary, to give practice in building a set of words with the same sound.

**Prepare:** Photocopy the picture on the next page several times and cut up to make separate carriages. Use one colour for each train.

- Use one onset and rime pattern for each train, e.g.

    Train 1 (red)      Rime = 'in'      The onset letters = 'p', 't', 's'.

    Train 2 (blue)      Rime = 'it'      The onset letters = 's', 'p', 'n', etc.

- Make four sets of three words and print the onset and the rime of a word on the reverse side of each card, as explained below.

**To play:** The rules for the game can be adapted to meet the individual needs of the pupils. The aim of the game is to complete a train.

Players win a train if they can read the words on the reverse side.

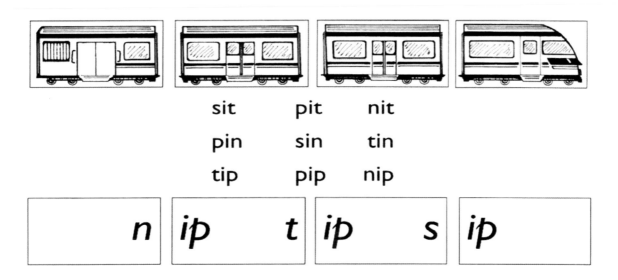

|      |      |      |
|------|------|------|
| sit  | pit  | nit  |
| pin  | sin  | tin  |
| tip  | pip  | nip  |

| n | ip | t | ip | s | ip |
|---|----|---|----|---|----|

 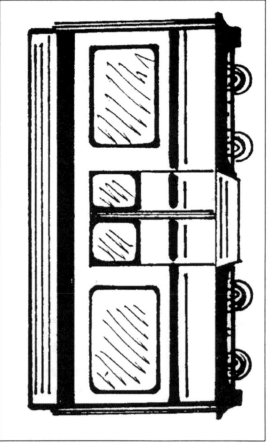

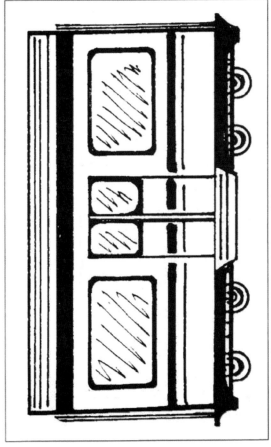 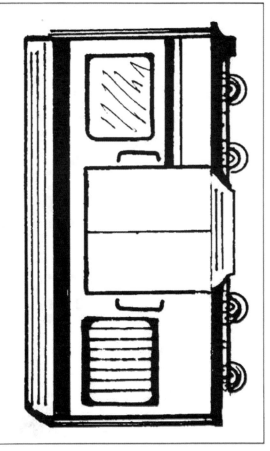

34

# Advanced Alphabetic Stage

## Game 1: 'Complete the word'

All games should be played in a flexible way to meet the needs and interests of the pupils.

They can be extended to secondary level for those having difficulty in learning to read and spell.

**Prepare:** Use a game board. The teacher and pupils can make various imaginative game boards, e.g. treasure island, race track, football.

- Make two sets of cards, one set for the rimes and one set for the matching onset letters.
- Use initial letters or blends – Set 1 ('t', 'p', 'n', 's', 'sp', 'sn').
- Print the 'rime' onto separate cards to fit the base boards for Bingo game, pages 36 and 37 – Set 2.
- Make 12 cards with 'in', 15 with 'it', and 15 with 'ip'.

**To play:** (group or individual)

### a) Reading game (visual)

- Place the cards face down in two packs, one for onset and one for rime.
- First player throws the dice and picks up a card from each pack.
- If a word can be made the player moves the number of spaces on the board.

### b) Spelling game (visual)

- Players look at the word on the onset and rime cards and read the words aloud. Then it is covered.
- The word is written down from memory and checked.

## Game 2: 'Bingo' as a reading game (auditory)

**To play:** Play Bingo using the base cards (on next page) and the rime cards for Set 2 from 'Complete the Word' above.

- The caller reads the rime card for the players to point to an onset letter on their base card.
- **OR** the caller reads the whole word and the first player who points to the onset letter and says the rime wins the card.

## Game 3: 'Bingo' as a spelling game (auditory)

**To play:** The caller shows the rime card and the players point to the onset letter on their card.

- Use the RSW (Reading and Spelling through Writing) routine (see page 45) and read, spell and write aloud the word.
- The pupils all write the word.
- The winner is the first to spell a target of 5 or 10 words.

**Complete the Word**      **BINGO**      **1**

| | | |
|---|---|---|
| sp _ | p _ | s _ |
| t _ | p _ | sn _ |

**Complete the Word**      **BINGO**      **2**

| | | |
|---|---|---|
| t _ | sp _ | n _ |
| s _ | p _ | sn _ |

**Complete the Word**      **BINGO**      **3**

| | | |
|---|---|---|
| n _ | t _ | p _ |
| sn _ | sp _ | s _ |

**Complete the Word**     BINGO     4

p _     n _     sn _

t _     s _     sp _

**Complete the Word**     BINGO     5

sn _     p _     s _

n _     t _     sp _

**Complete the Word**     BINGO     6

s _     sn _     sp _

p _     t _     n _

*good game – make it!*
x

## Game 4: 'Lucky dice – ladder game'

**Prepare:** Make base boards, larger than the samples below, with an onset letter on each rung of the 'ladder'.

- Laminate so that each ladder can be used several times for writing in the word with water soluble coloured felt pens (fine).

**To play: Spelling game.** Only put two rimes on base dice card, if pupils are at the beginning stage (see page 28).

- Pupils have one ladder each. First player throws a dice. If their number gives a rime that makes a word on their card, they spell and write it on that rung of the ladder.

| | |
|---|---|
| s —  | r — |
| d —  | b — |
| f —  | f — |
| j —  | g — |
| m —  | P — |
| b —  | s — |
| l —  | m — |
| n —  | l — |
| P —  | t — |
| t —  | d — |

| • | •• | •• | ••• | •• •• | ••• ••• |
|---|---|---|---|---|---|
| at | et | ot | ip | op | ug |

also good

## Game 5: 'Missing vowels ladder game'

Alternative 'Ladder luck' game using short vowels to complete the words.

- Use a dice card to win the missing vowels and insert to complete a word.

| p _ n | t _ p |
|---|---|
| n _ p | s _ t |
| n _ t | s _ n |
| sp _ n | sn _ p |

| • | •<br>• | •<br>•<br>• | •  •<br>•  • | •  •<br>•<br>•  • |
|---|---|---|---|---|
| a | e | i | o | u |

*The six on the dice allows the player to select any vowel sound s/he needs to complete a word.

### Game 6: 'Silent 'e' game'

**Prepare**: *Game for two. Make base boards, larger than the samples below. Make sets of letters to put into the spaces on the base boards, e.g. base boards for 'a – e' words ('made', 'tape', 'late', etc.) need enough small letters 'a' and 'e' to place in spaces.*

- *There are enough words for two boards to be made for each long vowel sound 'a', 'i', 'o', 'u'. There are insufficient one syllable words for 'e- e' base boards. (Refer to Word Lists from page 47.)*

**To play**: *Each child has a base board for the long vowel sound to be used.*

- *The vowel letter cards for the middle and ends of the words are placed face down on the table.*
- *First player turns over one card, but must return a silent 'e' card until a first medial vowel has been found.*
- *The word must be read each time, e.g. 'pip', then when the final 'e' is added they read 'pipe'. (Some children who have already learnt the silent 'e' rule still find this very difficult when playing the game.)*

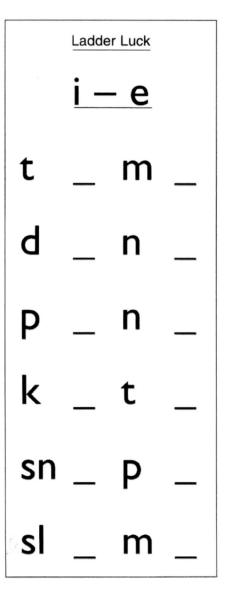

## Game 7: 'Pirate games'

**Prepare:** The game can be played using any groups of words to give reading practice. Practice in blending letters and reading words with initial, medial and final phonemes.

- 'Pirate games' can also be played to give practice in reading words with long vowel sounds and vowel digraphs.
- Make 7 sets of cards with 7 cards in a set. Make a 'Key' reference card for each game, e.g. -nd, -nt, -mp, see cards below. (See lists of words from p.47 etc.)

**To play:** Deal 7-10 cards to each player (depending on time available). Place remaining cards face down as a pool.

- Players place their cards face up and identify the blends as they sort them into similar sets.
- First player takes a card from the pool and placing it on the table, reads the word, Any cards may then be taken from other players with the same onset (e.g. 'sp', or 'sh') or rime (e.g. '-at', '-ick') used for the game, if the words can be read.
- The first to collect an agreed total number of cards wins.

| bent | bump | mend |
|------|------|------|
| went | slump | bend |
| tent | stump | |

# Advanced Alphabetic Stage (continued)

Children will continue to move through this stage as they learn to segment spoken words into chunks and units of sound with four or more phonemes. Words with a final assimilation (e.g. '-mp as in 'jump', '-nd' as in 'stand') may prove difficult to spell.

When they are able to read, write and spell one syllable words with short vowels they will be ready to move on to the first and second choice spellings for the long vowel sounds (see notes and word lists in Appendices, pp. 52-55), and multisyllabic words.

### Game 8:  'Snakes and ladders'
**To play:**  The sets of word families can be combined with each other for any board game for reading and spelling games.  Points are scored for reading the words correctly or for spelling and writing them down.

### Game 9:  'Odds and evens'
**To play:**  This game can be played where two word cards are spelt for an even number on the dice and one word for an odd number.

### Game 10:  'Race track'
**To play:**  Pupils will need practice in reading and spelling words with long vowel sounds.  A board game is invaluable for this exercise.  A game is only a *spelling* game when a pupil spells aloud and writes the words down.

At this advanced alphabetic stage, children will begin to develop an automatic response to sounds and their syllables.  Many pupils will need practice with alliteration and deleting syllables and phonemes in words.  Pupils with difficulties in blending sounds will benefit from practice in decoding non-words which can be introduced in a board game.

# The Orthographic Stage

The *initial orthographic stage* is introduced in '**Learning Can Be Fun**' – Book 2 (Word Attack Skills and Syllables).  However, notes and word lists for teaching long vowel spelling choices have been included in this book.

An *advanced orthographic stage* will be reached after the pupils are confident in spelling sight words and words with long vowels sounds.  They will also need to have an understanding of word patterns for suffixing and the use of morphemes, e.g. origins of word roots, prefixes and suffixes.

# Introduce a continuous cursive handwriting style from the start

Handwriting is a kinaesthetic motor movement and as this is a strong memory area of the brain it is very difficult to change a style once it has been established. The ball and stick movements of 'print' do not encourage a flowing movement as the pencil is lifted to write every letter; this increases the tendency to reverse or confuse letter shapes. Many children find it very difficult to change from a print style to cursive writing in the first two years of school and so should learn to write the cursive style of letters from the beginning.

1. Continuous cursive writing helps children with spatial difficulties as every letter begins on the line with an approach stroke and has a carry-on stroke that leads easily to the next letter. They do not have to think of where to start writing a letter.

2. Words are written as whole units helping children with problems of sequential order and direction to move from left to right across the page.

3. The continuous movement when writing and spelling a word avoids breaks in concentration, reversals and omission of letters.

4. It encourages a flowing movement across the page which eventually becomes an efficient, and legible, writing style leading to speed.

5. This style of cursive handwriting improves spelling but, as with all motor skills, it needs practice.

6. Pupils are taught that their pencil hold, the angle of the paper and the way they sit will all contribute to improve their handwriting style.

7. Many children need guidelines in the beginning stages. Talk them through the letter shapes as they write. They may also need to make large tactile movements using different materials (e.g. brush and water; sand, salt or bubble bath tray; or torch letters) to feel the letter shapes as they learn to write and remember them. Later they give the sounds or names of the letters, saying them aloud as they write.

8. These large whole-arm movements encourage the motor muscles from the hand, arm and shoulder to integrate with the brain. They are essential for children who have problems with spatial awareness and those in the early years, e.g. Reception and Year 1 (in the UK from 4 to 6 years).

9. This style of handwriting may be adapted easily to meet a school's handwriting policy but it should always be discussed with the Headteacher of a school before being introduced.

10. It is the key to multisensory learning for children with specific learning difficulties, e.g. those with reading and spelling problems (see example on next page from the 'Hickey Multisensory Language Course', 2nd edition 1992). It has been developed by Briggs, to be used in the classroom, with the multisensory RSW (Read, Spell and Write) sheets which help to reinforce and memorise the letter shapes.

Some letters follow similar patterns of movements and can be taught in the following groups. Follow the multisensory routine on the RSW sheets, e.g.

There are five 'up, down, off' letters:

*l  t  i  j  x*

There are five 'up, down, up again, over and off' letters:

*n  h  m  p  k*

There are seven 'over and back' letters:

*r  c  a  d  g  q  o  s*

There are five 'off the top' letters where the 'carry-on' stroke to the next letter comes off the top of the letter:

*b  o  r  v  w*

There are three 'up, down, up again, down again' letters:

*u  w  y*

There are five letters with **tails**. These must cross on the line:

*f  g  j  y  z*

There are four **alternative** style letters:

*b  x  z  p*

44

## Read, Write and Spell (R.W.S.) Sheets

## Multisensory writing practice

Use your hand to feel the letter shape, your eyes to look carefully and to remember how the shape is made, your voice to give the sound and name of the letter, and your ears to remember the sound as you say and write the letter.

**Remember: Always start on the line.**

| | Copy the letter giving the sound and name **aloud**. |
|---|---|
| In this first box trace the letter giving the sound and the name as you write. Talk through the letter shape first. Trace the letter several times using different colours to learn the shape.  | |
| Cover the letters above and write from memory. | Put your pencil on the paper. Eyes closed. Try to visualise and feel the shape as you write the letter |

/

^

/

^

/

^

/

^

/

^

/

^

## APPENDIX 1.   Word lists for blending letters in V C words
### - initial and final blends for onset and rime

*Order of first letters introduced* – **s, a, n, d, p, i, t / h, e, c, k, b, r, m, l**

| at | ap | an | ad | am | Irregular words |
|---|---|---|---|---|---|
| pat | tap | pan | had | Pam | the |
| sat | nap | can | Dad | Sam | as |
| spat | sap | Dan | sad | dam | this |
| hat | snap | Ann | mad | ham | with |
| cat | cap | Stan | pad | ram | am |
| bat | map | tan | lad | | I |
| rat | lap | man | bad | | have |
| fat | | ran | | | is |
| | | | | | into |
| | | | | | they |

| it | ip | in | id | im |
|---|---|---|---|---|
| sit | sip | din | did | him |
| pit | tip | pin | lid | slim |
| nit | Pip | tin | hid | Tim |
| Blue tit | nip | sin | rid | dim |
| spit | snip | spin | kid | |
| | Dip | | bid | |

| ant | and |
|---|---|
| pant | hand |
| | sand |
| | stand |
| | band |

## Notes 1. – 'Reading, Spelling and Writing' letters and words

1. Introduce each phoneme of the 'sandpit' letters.  Make words using magnetic letters.  Put words into sentences.  Teach pupils to write letters in cursive style from Reception Year. (See page 44 for example of writing style.)
2. Use a photocopied sheet of A4 paper divided into 4 parts with writing guidelines in each section (see RSW sheets, pages 45).
3. Use the RSW sheet (Read, Spell, Write) and follow the multisensory routine to trace, copy, write from memory and then write the letter with eyes closed.  This is only effective if the pupils voice the sound and the name of the letter **ALOUD** as they write.
4. If necessary use kinaesthetic large movements before this stage with sand or salt tray, large paint brush and water on a rough wall, or a 'Magna Doodle' board.
5. Make a set of A5 demonstration 'Write and Spell Cards'.  As each phoneme is introduced add it to the pack for daily writing practice showing the pupils the printed letter on the face of the card in brackets and the written cursive example on the reverse side of the card.
6. First spelling words and tricky words can also be learnt using the RSW sheet.

## APPENDIX 2.

*Order of letters introduced –* **f, o, j, g, u, y, w, qu, v, x**

| -et | -en | -est | | Irregular words |
|-----|-----|------|---|-----------------|
| pet | pen | test | | there |
| jet | ten | pest | | come |
| net | hen | best | | some |
| let | men | rest | | do |
| set | | | | does |
| get | | | | done |
| bet | | | | one |
| wet | | | | once |
| met | | | | he |
| | | | | be |

| -ent | -end | -ed | y | we |
|------|------|-----|---|-----|
| tent | tend | bed | yes | are |
| rent | send | Ted | yet | friend |
| sent | spend | red | yen | ton |
| went | bend | shed | | son |
| spent | mend | fed | | won |
| bent | | | | to |
| | | | | too |

| -ot | -op | -od | -ob |
|-----|-----|-----|-----|
| tot | top | pod | sob |
| spot | shop | cod | snob |
| not | stop | sod | hob |
| dot | flop | God | mob |
| pot | pop | nod | rob |
| rot | mop | hod | cob |
| hot | hop | | yob |
| lot | crop | | |

## Notes 2. – Initial and final blends, writing sentences, punctuation

1. Some pupils will have no difficulty with initial and final blends. It is not necessary to add these spellings to the RSW pack. A reading pack of initial and final blends can be made for those who need more practice.
2. The pupils write and spell as they think of the words in a family, e.g. 'sp'. The words can make a story or picture which helps the pupils to visualize each word family and group.
3. They then see how many words they can write in a 'silly' sentence.
4. At this stage concentrate on sentence structure and punctuation, e.g. capital letters and full stops. Play the Bingo and Pirates games for reading practice.
5. Sentences are dictated by the teacher in the following lesson.

# APPENDIX 3. Words with 's' blends, 'l' blends and 'r' blends

| sp | sn | st | sc | sk | sl |
|---|---|---|---|---|---|
| spin | snip | Stan | scan | skin | slip |
| span | snap | stand | scamp | skimp | slap |
| spend | snub | stamp | scuff | skit | slop |
| spud | snag | stag | scum | skim | slag |
| spot | snug | stop | scab | skid | slog |
| spit | snack | step | | skill | slug |
| spill | sniff | stun | | skiff | slim |
| spell | | stick | | skint | slum |
| speck | | stack | | sky | slot |
| spent | | stock | | skip | slack |
| spoon | | stuck | | | slam |
| spy | | still | | | slick |

| pl | bl | cl | gl | fl | spl |
|---|---|---|---|---|---|
| plan | blot | clip | glad | flat | splash |
| plug | black | clap | glum | flan | splat |
| plot | block | clop | glut | flop | |
| plop | blush | clan | glug | flick | |
| plush | blink | club | | fleck | |
| plod | | clamp | | flap | |
| pluck | | clump | | flock | |
| plum | | clod | | flag | |
| plump | | cloth | | flab | |
| plank | | clog | | fly | |
| plant | | clot | | flank | |
| | | clam | | flash | |
| | | cling | | fling | |

| pr | tr | dr | br | cr | gr |
|---|---|---|---|---|---|
| pram | trap | drop | brick | crab | grip |
| prop | trim | dry | brat | cry | grub |
| prod | trip | drip | brag | crib | grab |
| prompt | try | drab | brand | crack | grump |
| prick | trad | dram | bring | cramp | grand |
| pry | tramp | dreg | brink | crag | grant |
| prank | trek | drat | | cram | grid |
| | track | drum | | crumb | grasp |
| | trod | drag | | crunch | grit |
| | trump | drill | | crush | grim |
| | tram | drift | | crimp | Greg |
| | trunk | drunk | | | |
| | | drink | | | |
| | | drug | | | |

## Words with 'r' blends continued:

| fr | str | spr |
|---|---|---|
| frog | strap | spry |
| fry | strength | sprint |
| from | strip | sprig |
| frock | string | spring |
| Frank | strong | sprung |
| | strand | sprang |

## APPENDIX 4.  Final Assimilated Blends (-nd, -nt, -mp, -nk, -nch)

1. Pupils who have difficulty in hearing these final blends when spelling words may have auditory discrimination or short-term memory problems.
2. They will need more practice and time with reading and spelling games.
3. Continue the same RSW procedure as in the previous notes.

| -and | -end | -ind | -ond | -und |
|---|---|---|---|---|
| sand | bend | bind | bond | fund |
| land | fend | kind | fond | |
| band | lend | mind | pond | |
| strand | mend | rind | frond | |
| hand | send | blind | | |
| stand | (friend) | wind | | |
| grand | spend | find | | |
| brand | | hind | | |
| rand | | | | |

| -amp | -emp | -imp | -omp | -ump |
|---|---|---|---|---|
| stamp | hemp | limp | stomp | slump |
| ramp | | wimp | romp | dump |
| camp | | | pomp | stump |
| cramp | | | | hump |
| damp | | | | bump |
| scamp | | | | jump |
| lamp | | | | lump |
| tramp | | | | pump |

| -st | -sh | -nch | -ink | -ank |
|---|---|---|---|---|
| bust | ash | bench | sink | bank |
| test | bash | trench | blink | plank |
| rust | cash | stench | link | dank |
| chest | dash | bunch | mink | stank |
| crust | gash | hunch | rink | thank |
| vest | mash | lunch | slink | hank |
| trust | sash | munch | drink | prank |
| crest | rash | crunch | brink | clank |

| must | crash | inch | stink | drank |
|------|-------|------|-------|-------|
| pest | flash | flinch | wink | rank |
| dust | trash | winch | pink | flank |
| quest | clash |  |  | sank |
| gust | gush |  | **-unk** |  |
| best | hush |  | sunk |  |
| just | mush |  | junk |  |
| nest | rush |  | trunk |  |
| fist | blush |  | bunk |  |
| west | flush |  | hunk |  |
| mist | slush |  |  |  |
| wrist | plush |  |  |  |
| twist | brush |  |  |  |
|  | crush |  |  |  |
|  | mesh |  |  |  |
|  | swish |  |  |  |
|  | fish |  |  |  |
|  | dish |  |  |  |
|  | wish |  |  |  |
|  | (push) |  |  |  |
|  | (bush) |  |  |  |

## APPENDIX 5.

### After one short vowel 'c' musk go with 'k'

Use the 1, 2, 3, Rule – Count from the first vowel and 'k' must always be the third letter.

| -ick | -ack | -eck | -ock | (-uck) |
|------|------|------|------|--------|
| tick | tack | peck | tock | tuck |
| sick | sack | speck | sock | suck |
| pick | pack | neck | dock | buck |
| stick | stack | heck | stock | stuck |
| brick | rack | wreck | rock | duck |
| kick | crack | deck | lock | muck |
| ticket | packet | check | rocket | bucket |

| -ing | -ang | -eng | -ong | -ung |
|------|------|------|------|------|
| sing | sang | length | song | sung |
| string | tang | strength | strong | strung |
| bring | bang |  | dong | dung |
| ring | rang |  | pong | hung |
| sting | hang |  | prong | bung |
| fling | fang |  | long | flung |
| sling | slang |  | wrong | slung |
| thing | gang |  |  | rung |
| sting | prang |  |  | stung |
| swing |  |  |  |  |

51

## One syllable words need two 'll's

| -all | -ill | -ell | -ull | -oll |
|------|------|------|------|------|
| ball | bill | bell | gull | doll |
| call | frill | fell | hull | |
| fall | fill | hell | dull | |
| hall | shrill | sell | | |
| wall | hill | smell | ('almost, 'always' | |
| stall | spill | swell | have one 'l' in a two | |
| | still | spell | syllable word) | |
| | kill | | | |
| | pill | | | |
| | sill | | | |

| qu | wa | squ | (ŏŏ) | (ōō) |
|------|------|------|------|------|
| quit | was | squad | hook | hoot |
| quick | wash | squash | book | boot |
| quill | want | squat | cook | root |
| quilt | wand | | look | fool |
| quiet | wasp | | crook | pool |
| quell | wad | | nook | stool |
| quad | what | | took | soon |
| quack | | | rook | moon |
| | | | soot | noon |
| | | | foot | spoon |
| | | | | hoop |
| | | | | loop |
| | | | | spook |

| Middle ee | End ee | Middle ar | | End ar | ar+e |
|-----------|--------|-----------|------|--------|------|
| meet | tree | hard | yard | car | care |
| sheep | bee | harp | dark | jar | bare |
| sweep | flee | sharp | park | bar | fare |
| sweet | see | card | bark | far | scare |
| keep | fee | tart | mark | tar | stare |
| steep | (knee) | start | shark | scar | rare |
| greet | | cart | spark | star | dare |
| street | | smart | lark | | hare |
| sheet | | part | scarf | | mare |
| teeth | | dart | snarl | | |
| Queen | | yarn | | | |
| seen | | darn | | | |
| feel | | barn | | | |
| creep | | harm | | | |
| sleep | | farm | | | |

**Two syllables:**  garden    sharpen    harden    market    parking

farmer    carpet    garment    bargain    darken

| th | sh | ch | wh |
|---|---|---|---|
| this | ship | chip | who |
| then | shop | chop | what |
| there | shut | chat | when |
| thing | shall | chart | why |
| these | should | charge | where |
| think | shout | chunk | which |
| thick | shock | chunk | while |
| their | shed | change | |
| thumb | shake | chick | |

| tch | | dge | g+u |
|---|---|---|---|
| catch | itch | edge | guess |
| hatch | witch | hedge | guest |
| batch | hitch | wedge | guy |
| patch | ditch | ledge | guide |
| scratch | bitch | fudge | guilty |
| wretch | stitch | budge | rogue |
| sketch | scotch | badge | vague |
| fetch | hutch | ridge | |
| (except – much | | fridge | |
| such | which | dodge | |
| rich | | | |

## APPENDIX 6.  Long vowel spellings and vowel digraphs

1. There is a structured way of teaching long vowel spellings.  Introduce the high frequency spellings as 'first choice' spellings of the long vowel sounds.  Then introduce the second choice spellings when the first choice words are established for each long vowel.  A long vowel says the name of the letter.  It may be heard at the end of an open syllable ('to-tal'), or in a word with a silent 'e' at the end ('home'), or with a vowel digraph ('snow' or 'goat').

2. Children with specific learning difficulties (dyslexia) need a clear teaching plan as they find vowel digraphs very difficult to master in one syllable words.  These need to be taught step by step:

   **Step 1.** Teach 'vowel consonant e' words first ('a–e', 'i–e', 'o–e', 'u–e').  The line between the vowels refers to the consonant which changes but the word pattern 'VCe' remains the same (e.g. t i m e, p i p e, s t i l e, w i n e, t i d e).  There are few spellings with 'e–e' in one syllable words and so 'ee' becomes the first choice spelling for long vowel sound 'e' (e.g. teeth, queen).

**Step 2.** Word endings may then be introduced (e.g. '-ay', '-y', '-ee', '-ow', '-ew').

**Step 3.** The second choice spellings (e.g. 'ea', 'igh', 'oa', 'ai', 'eu') are introduced when the pupil is confident in spelling the first choice words. Avoid teaching 'ai' too early as this phoneme involves the use of homophones (e.g. sail, sale).

3. A chart can be built up so that pupils can review their progress. (See Hickey.)

4. The reading and spelling games in this book will provide reinforcement at every stage of learning. Follow the same RSW routine (page 45) when learning to spell the words and include the use of visualisation techniques.

## First choice spellings in one syllable words

| a–e | | i–e | | o–e | | u–e |
|---|---|---|---|---|---|---|
| came | cape | time | ride | hope | rode | tune |
| same | tape | grime | pipe | rope | home | dune |
| tame | cane | slime | ripe | slope | vote | June |
| game | lane | dine | tripe | cope | dote | mule |
| cake | mane | fine | snipe | mope | note | rule |
| make | vane | line | kite | robe | tote | cube |
| bake | made | pine | bite | bone | yoke | tube |
| take | wade | spine | quite | tone | | rude |
| lake | late | wine | | cone | | cute |
| wake | rate | tide | | phone | | fuse |
| tale | mate | wide | | lone | | fluke |
| male | gate | side | | throne | | plume |
| sale | fate | slide | | code | | |
| gale | | hide | | mode | | |

## First choice endings

| -ay | -y | -ow | -ew |
|---|---|---|---|
| play | try | snow | stew |
| slay | spy | grow | grew |
| tray | fry | flow | slew |
| stay | cry | blow | drew |
| lay | fly | row | brew |
| may | dry | low | few |
| bay | why | bow | crew |
| spray | by | mow | dew |
| say | my | tow | new |
| day | sly | know | knew |
| way | pry | throw | threw |
| jay | sty | crow | |
| ray | shy | sow | |
| hay | | | |

## Second choice spellings

| ai | ea | igh | oa | ie | ey | oe |
|------|-------|--------|-------|-----|------|------|
| tail | sea | might | boat | pie | they | toe |
| sail | beach | right | stoat | die | grey | hoe |
| rail | each | knight | float | tie | obey | sloe |
| hail | teach | fight | goat | lie | prey | |
| fail | tea | sight | moat | | | |
| gain | cream | tight | moan | | | |
| Spain | meat | flight | toad | | | |
| rain | peach | bright | road | | | |
| pain | peas | light | soak | | | |
| main | seat | night | foal | | | |
| | beat | | soap | | | |
| | reach | | loan | | | |
| | | | goal | | | |
| | | | toast | | | |
| | | | coast | | | |
| | | | boast | | | |
| | | | roast | | | |

## Vowel digraphs

| oi | oy | ou | ow | au | aw | ei |
|-------|-------|----------|-------|-----------|---------|---------|
| boil | toy | sound | bow | haunt | paw | eight |
| foil | boy | found | cow | sauce | saw | weight |
| toil | enjoy | mound | now | author | law | freight |
| spoil | annoy | ground | row | Paul | claw | |
| join | | shout | sow | Autumn | jaw | |
| coin | | about | town | August | awful | |
| | | hound | gown | audience | straw | |
| | | house | clown | automatic | flaw | |
| | | mouse | | | gnaw | |
| | | mountain | | | Jackdaw | |

## Vowel + 'r' words

| er | ir | ur | our | ear |
|--------|---------|-------|---------|------------|
| her | dirty | hurt | colour | early |
| term | thirty | purse | flavour | pearl |
| germ | flirt | burn | favour | earthquake |
| jumper | thirsty | curl | | learn |
| stern | girl | hurl | | heard |
| fern | twirl | | | |
| | skirt | | | |
| | shirt | | | |
| | fir | | | |
| | stir | | | |
| | bird | | | |

## APPENDIX 7.

## 'W' rules

'wa'    'What was that wasp doing?'

'war'   'War words'

'wor'   'The worst word in the world is work!'

## Soft 'c' plus 'e', 'i', 'y'

## Soft 'g' plus 'e', 'i', 'y'

## Suffixes:  A suffix means action when it is added to the end of a word

- All words have patterns which are marked from the first vowel to the next vowel.

- These word patterns need to be easily recognised in base one syllable words before introducing the suffixing rules.

- The base word patterns are V.C., V.C.C., V.C.e, V.V.C and V.V.

## Game

- Make a pack of cards with these base words with 7-9 cards for each pattern, e.g. 'hop' = V.C., 'jump' = V.C.C., 'look' = V.V.C.

- Encourage the children to sort the cards.  Play games with the cards, e.g. 'Three of a kind', etc. before introducing the suffixing rules.

- The vowel suffixes are -ed, -ing, -er, -y, -est.

## The rules are double, add, drop, or change

i)   You only **double** a consonant after a V.C. base word, e.g. hop + ing = hopping.

ii)  You **add** a suffix to V.C.V., V.V.C. words and words ending in V.V.

iii) You **drop** the 'e' before 'ing' and when another vowel can do its work.

iv)  You **change** the 'I' to 'y' when there is a consonant before the 'y'.

(Refer to the 'Hickey Multisensory Language Course' for a more detailed structured approach to learning to spell.)

# Resources

## Recommended materials:

a) 'The Hickey Multisensory Language Course' (3rd Edition, 2000) Ed. Combley. Wiley. Available from SEN Marketing: www.senbooks.co.uk.

b) 'Alpha to Omega: The A-Z of teaching, reading, writing and spelling' (6th Edition, 2006), Hornsby, Shear & Pool, available from www.senbooks.co.uk.

c) 'Before Alpha: Learning games for the under fives' (3rd Edition, 1996), Hornsby. Available from SEN Marketing; www.senbooks.co.uk.

d) 'Edith Norrie Letter Case', available from the Helen Arkell Dyslexia Centre: www.arkellcentre.org.uk.

e) Magnetic lower case plastic letters. Available in tubs from the Early Learning Centre: www.elc.co.uk.

f) Blank Playing Cards are available in packs of 100 (or 5 x 100) from SEN Marketing: www.senbooks.co.uk.

g) LDA Learning: www.ldalearning.com.

h) Phonic Activities 1 and 2 – Brighter Vision Publications.

i) The 'Spelling Made Easy' Series, Brand. Available from SEN Marketing: www.senbooks.co.uk and Egon Publishers Ltd: www.egon.co.uk.


## Testing materials for SpLD:

a) A whole variety of products for different situations: www.lucid-research.com.

b) Dyslexia Screening Tests, various levels, Fawcett & Nicholson (2nd Edition), Pearson: www.psychcorp.co.uk.

c) Phonological Assessment Battery: GL Assessment: www.gl-assessment.co.uk.

d) Phonological Awareness Procedure: Tests, Gorrie & Parkinson, 1995. STASS Publications: www.stasspublications.co.uk.

# Bibliography

Adams, M.J. (1990) *Beginning to Read*. London: MIT Press.

Augur, J. & Briggs, S. (1992) *Hickey Multisensory Language Course* – 2nd Edition. London: Whurr.

Ball, E. & Balchman, B. (1998) 'Phoneme segmentation training: effect on reading readiness'. *Annals of Dyslexia – Orton Dyslexia Society 38*, pp.208 -222.

Blachman, B. (Ed.) (1997). *Foundations of Reading Acquisition and Dyslexia: Implications for Early Intervention*. Mahwah, N.J.: Earlbaum.

Bourassa, D. & Treiman, R. (2003) 'Spelling in children with dyslexia: Analyses from the Treiman-Bourassa Early Spelling Test'. *Scientific Studies of Reading 7*, pp.309-333.

Bradley, L. & Bryant, P. (1978) 'Difficulties in auditory organisation as a possible cause of reading backwardness'. *Nature 271*, pp.746 – 747.

Bryant, P. et al, (1996) 'Reason, rhyme and reading'. *Child Education*, pp.11-13.

Foy, J.G. & Mann, V.A. (2003) 'Phonological Awareness, Speech Development and Letter Knowledge in Preschool Children'. *Annals of Dyslexia, Vol. 53*, 2003, p.166.

Frith, U. (1985) 'Beneath the surface of developmental dyslexia'. Patterson, K. & Coltheart, M. (Eds.) *Surface Dyslexia*. London: Routledge and Kegan Paul.

Frost, J. & Lonnegaard, A. (1997) *Sproglege*. Translated by Feilker, D. as *Language Games* (quoted by Frost at UKRA Conference, Cobham, Surrey, 1998).

Gillon, G.T. (2004) *Phonological Awareness – From Research to Practice.* Guilford Press: New York.

Goswami, U. & Bryant, P. (1990) *Phonological Skills and Learning to Read*. Hove, UK: Laurence Erlbaum.

Goswami, U. (1996) 'Rhyme and Analogy'. *Child Education*, pp.28-29.

Gough, P., Ehri, L. & Treiman, R. (Eds.) *Reading Acquisition*, pp.56-106. New Jersey: Erlbaun.

Liberman, I. et al (1974) 'Explicit syllable and phoneme segmentation in the young child'. *Journal of Experimental Child Psychology 18*, pp.201-212.

Liberman, I. et al (1989) 'The alphabetic principle and learning to read'. Shankweiler, D. & Liberman, I. (Eds.) *Phonology and Reading Disability*. Ann Arbor: University of Michigan Press, pp.1-34.

Lindamood, P. et al (1997) 'Achieving competence in language and literacy by training in phonemic awareness, concept imagery and comparator function'. Hulme, C. & Snowling, M. (Eds.) *Dyslexia – Biology, Cognition and Intervention*. London: Whurr.

Lundberg, I. Forst, J. & Petersen, O. (1988) 'Effects of an extensive program for stimulating phonological awareness in pre-school children'. _Reading Research Quarterly 23_, pp.263-284.

Muter, V. (1994) 'Influence of phonological awareness and letter knowledge on beginning reading and spelling development'. Hulme, C. & Snowling, M. (Eds.) _Reading Development and Dyslexia_. London: Whurr.

Muter, V. (2005) 'Language, Phonology and Beginning to Read, (Assessment)', _The Dyslexia Handbook,_ p. 153. British Dyslexia Association.

Reynell, J. (1977) _The Reynell Developmental Language Scales_. Windsor: NFER.

Reynell, J. (1978) _Helping Language Development: A Developmental Programme for Children with Early Language Handicaps_. London: Edward Arnold.

Shaywitz, S. (2003). 'Overcoming dyslexia: a new and complete science-based program for reading problems at any level'. _Annals of Dyslexia, 2003, Vol. 53_, p.6. New York: Alfred A. Knopf.

Snow, C., Griffin, P. & Burns, S. (2005) 'Knowledge to support the teaching of reading: Preparing teachers for a changing world'. _Annals of Dyslexia, 2006, Vol. 56, No. 1_ p.76. San Francisco, Jossey-Bass.

Snowling, J. & Nation, K. (1997) 'Language phonology and learning to read'. Hulme, C. & Snowling, M. (Eds.) _Dyslexia: Biology, Cognition and Intervention_. London: Whurr.

Snowling, M. (1987) _Dyslexia: A Cognitive Development Perspective_. Oxford: Blackwell.

Snowling, M., Goulandris, N. & Stackhouse, S. (1994) 'Phonological constraints on learning to read: evidence from single case studies of reading difficulty'. Hulme, C. & Snowling, M. (Eds.) _Reading Development and Dyslexia_. London: Whurr, pp.182-211.

Snowling, M. (1995) 'Phonological processing and developmental dyslexia, which responds to early intervention'. _Journal of Research in Reading 18_, pp.132-138.

Snowling, M. (1996) 'Dyslexia: A hundred years on – a verbal not a visual disorder, which responds to early intervention'. _BMJ Volume 318_.

Snowling, M.J. & Hayiou-Thomas, M.E. (2006) 'The dyslexia spectrum: Continuities between reading, speech and language impairments'. Topics in Language Disorders, 26, pp.108-124. _Annals of Dyslexia, 2006, Vol. 56._ No.2 p.229.

Stackhouse, J. & Wells, B. (1997) 'How do speech and language problems affect literacy development' in Hulme, C. & Snowling, M. (Eds.) _Dyslexia: Biology, Cognition and Intervention_, London: Whurr, pp.182-211.

Torgesen, J.K. (2000) 'Individual differences in responses to early intervention reading'. _Learning disabilities, 1,_ p.55-64. Research and Practice.

Treiman, R. (1985) 'Onsets and rimes as units of spoken syllables: evidence from children'. _Journal of Experimental Psychology 33_, pp.161-181.

Treiman, R. (1992) _'The Role of intrasyllabic units in learning to read and spell'._

Treiman, R. (1997, 2002). _Annals of Dyslexia, 2003 Vol. 53_, p.147.

Vellutino, F. (1979) _Dyslexia – Theory and Research_, London: MIT Press.

Vellutino, F. et al (1997) 'Cognitive profiles of difficult to remediate and readily remediated poor readers: toward distinguishing between constitutionally and experientially based causes of reading disability'. _Journal of Educational Psychology_, (quoted by Stanovich at the International Conference of Dyslexia, York, UK 1997).

Wagner, R. & Torgesen, J. (1987) 'The nature of phonological processing and its causal role in the acquisition of reading skills'. _Psychological Bulletin 101_, pp.192-212.

Wolf, M., Miller, L. & Donnelly, K. (2000) 'Retrieval, automaticity, vocabulary elaboration, orthography (RAVR-O): A comprehensive, fluency-based reading intervention program'. _Journal of Learning Disabilities, 33_, pp.375-386.

## Further Reading

The following books are available from SEN Marketing: www.senbooks.co.uk.

Gathercole, S. E. & Alloway, T. (2008) _Working Memory and Learning: a practical guide for teachers_. Sage: London.

Hulme, C. & Snowling, M.J. (2009) _Developmental Disorders of Language Learning and Cognition._ Wiley-Blackwell: Chichester.

MacKay, N. (2005) _Removing Dyslexia as a Barrier to Achievement_. SEN Marketing: Wakefield.

Nicolson, R. & Fawcett, A. (2008) _Dyslexia, Learning and the Brain_. MIT Press: Cambridge, USA.

Ott, P. (2006) _Teaching Children with Dyslexia: a practical guide_. Routledge: London

Reid, G. (2009) _Dyslexia: a practitioner's handbook_ 4th Edition. Wiley-Blackwell: Chichester.

Reid, G. (2009) _Routledge Companion to Dyslexia_. Routledge: Oxford.